CELEBRATING

LENT & EASTER
Book 2

DONALD HILTON

FESTIVAL SERVICES for the Church Year

Other books by Donald Hilton

Boy into Man
Girl into Woman
Celebrating Series
Six Men and a Pulpit
Risks of Faith
Raw Materials of Faith
Results of Faith
After Much Discussion

Compiled by Donald Hilton

Fresh Voices
A Word in Season
Prayers for the Church Community
(with Roy Chapman)

Published by:
National Christian Education Council
Robert Denholm House
Nutfield
Redhill, RH1 4HW

British Library Cataloguing-in-Publication Data:
Celebrating Lent & Easter.
Bk.2.
1. Christian Church. Holy Week & Lenten services – Rites
I. Hilton, Donald, *1932* – II. National Christian Education Council
264'

ISBN 0-7197-0690-4

© 1990 Donald Hilton

Typeset by One and A Half Graphics, Redhill, Surrey
Printed by Halstan & Co Ltd, Amersham, Buckinghamshire

PREFACE

This is one of a series of books offering Festival Services for use in local churches. *Celebrating Lent & Easter Book 2* contains four services: two for use on Sundays in Lent, one for Palm Sunday, and one for Easter Day. They are based on ideas which have been tested out in local churches and most if not all age-groups in the church can be involved. At their best, Festival Services are celebrations by the whole church family for the whole church family.

The services will be found most useful where the leader of worship gathers together those who work with the various age-groups in order to ensure full co-operation. The services should be altered and adapted in the light of local needs and opportunities. A brief rehearsal for those taking part will always be helpful. Use the opportunity to time, and where necessary adjust, the content of the service.

No place is given in the orders of service for either the Lord's Prayer or an offertory. These can be inserted according to local custom.

Leeds 1990   Donald Hilton

CONTENTS

3

WHAT DOES GOD WANT?

Introduction

This service is suitable for any Sunday in Lent, especially early in the period. It would be most useful where churches are willing to give 1-2 hours to a pattern of worship and education. It could form the programme for a Sunday morning or afternoon event, or a special Lenten weekday evening.

It is an all-age event and begins with a short act of worship. Then each person elects to join one of four groups. Three are educational/activity groups, the fourth follows a pattern of traditional worship. After an appropriate period the four groups unite for a final act of worship. The flexible approach allows groups to begin some of their work before the event or complete it afterwards.

The Theme

Although with a strong sense of God's call, Jesus was never on 'automatic pilot' as he sought to achieve God's purpose. Thoughtful-ness, discovery, learning, and prayer all formed part of his search for the will of God. Two events show this acutely – the Temptations (Luke 4. 1-13), and the Garden of Gethsemane (Luke 22. 39-46). The two events are different however. The Temptations sound like a summary in story form of thoughts and ideas worked out over a long period; the Garden of Gethsemane experience records a specific event. Both experiences are seminal for Jesus' ministry and our discipleship, and are the two foci of this service which gives all ages in the congregation a chance to reflect on life and faith, and make a Lenten commitment to God's purposes.

Preparation

As each member of the congregation will be able to choose from several possibilities, the style of worship and learning to follow (see later notes), tell the congregation about the groups well before the day so that their choice can be informed. Leaders, who should meet in advance to prepare the event, must be appointed for each group. They should also think about the concluding worship and consider appointing a further person to visit each group, find out what people are doing, and how it can be used in the concluding worship.

The Festival Service

Calls to worship *An older person should read the first, a teenager the second*
Matthew the gospel writer wrote:
> When he came to the territory of Caesarea Philippi, Jesus asked his disciples, 'Who do men say that the Son of Man is?' They answered: 'Some say John the Baptist, others Elijah, others Jeremiah, or one of the prophets'. 'And you,' he asked, 'who do you say I am?'

An 11 year old boy wrote:
> If Jesus was born today
> Would he come in the same way?
> What he be kind and heal the blind?
> Or would he make them pay?
> Would he be a rock star or maybe an artist?
> Or would he get married and settle down in a big house?
> If Jesus was around do you think people might notice him and listen to him or just walk away and think he was dumb?

Leader The ministry and life of Jesus always makes people think – about him, about themselves, and about the meaning of life. That is the purpose of this service. We will look at two special times in the life of Jesus when he struggled and thought deeply about life's purpose. His example will excite our own thoughtfulness.

Hymn Ye fair green hills of Galilee

Prayer
> Guide us, O God, in our worship so that our minds and hearts are open to new truth and insights.
> Give us the attentive mind, ready to hear new ideas and test them out against our own measured experience.

Give us the open mind so that we never imagine we know it all and can learn no new thing.

Give to us an eager mind ready to grapple with new truth, to be excited by life's discoveries, and ever seeking to expand our present horizons.

Give us a mind that can balance the good things of tradition and your new gifts for today, and be thankful for both. In the name of Jesus Christ, our Lord.   Amen

Leader In the days of Jesus people believed they knew what 'Messiah' meant. It described, they thought, the man God would choose as his special agent to solve the problems of the nation.

He would, some thought, be a warrior king who would rally the fighting men of the nations and drive the Roman army, which had invaded them, out of their country. Others thought he would be a man who would obey every one of the rules and regulations that the religious leaders had invented. Others hoped for someone who would have great spiritual power, able to revitalise the faith of their time. As a young man Jesus must have been involved in the discussion and argument.

Slowly the conviction grew on Jesus that he himself had a special task to do in God's name. He believed God had chosen him. But for what? Should he be a warrior king? Should he be a religious perfectionist keeping the rules and laws absolutely? Our Bible reading captures three of the ideas that came to Jesus over the years. Luke writes about them as though the Devil was talking to Jesus. Listen to the ideas and see how Jesus rejects all three.

Bible reading Luke 4.1-13

The Leader reminds the congregation of the four groups and invites each person to move to the chosen group.

Groups 1 – 3

Each group takes one of the following themes:

Group 1   How does God want us to use our lives?
Group 2   How do we make the world more like God's kingdom?
Group 3   What is the real job of the Church?

The Group leaders will have decided on the methods to be used to explore each of the themes. They might include:

● Writing poetry or hymns to a known tune. To save time someone may need to begin the task in advance, leaving the group or individuals to complete it.

- Producing a collage of pictures, quotations and comment.
- Finding quotations from anthologies appropriate to the theme.
- Writing a job specification for a Christian life, or for a local church.
- Identifying local projects, schemes, or problems in the community which the church ought to initiate, support, or seek to solve.
- Writing prayers on the theme.
- Discussing the theme and producing an article for the church magazine.
- Detailed Bible Study on either of the two Bible readings.

Throughout the work the groups should bear in mind 'the temptations' of Jesus when he was seeking the purpose of God, and the nature of his ministry. How does the Servant serve? What does Jesus' experience say to us in our search for God's purpose?

The group leaders must decide what aspect of the work written can be offered in the final worship; e.g. a new hymn written up on a blackboard, a collage interpreted, a prayer offered. Unfinished tasks can be completed during the following week, and in consultation with the usual leader of worship, used on subsequent Sundays.

Group 4 *This group follows a traditional pattern of worship as given below*

Hymn I can picture Jesus toiling

Bible reading Luke 22. 39-46

Sermon

Recap on the significance of the earlier reading showing Jesus working out the meaning of Messiahship against the background of people's expectations about the Messiah.

We know what he rejected. We need the rest of the gospels to show what he accepted. He interpreted Messiahship as the acceptance of love no matter what the cost in terms of poverty, suffering and pain.

Move to the Gethsemane story as another critical example of Jesus struggling to discover the will of God. The tension lies between his acknowledgement of human weakness (If it is possible take this cup away) and his commitment to God, no matter what the consequences. (Nonetheless your will not mine be done).

Gethsemane is not an example of 'the uncertainty of doubt' but of the 'uncertainty of faith'. What is its message to us as we seek to be disciples, as we work for a better world, and as we seek to offer the life of the Church to God?

Prayer

> Lord, in a world of indecision and choice, help us to choose the right way rather the wrong;
>
> At times in life when many paths lie before us, help us to make thoughtful decisions;
>
> In an age when so many voices are powerful and persuasive, help us to discriminate, weighing up the words of others;
>
> Living within the inevitable tensions of humanity, forgive us when we make mistakes, and show us how to start again with renewed confidence.
>
> And in all things may we see service to others and love of your truth as the most important things in our lives.

Hymn   When my love to God grows weak.

The four groups come together.

Concluding worship

Brief consultation will be needed to create the order of service. If the event is stretching over a period longer than the usual hour, refreshments can be served.

The inevitable sense of spontaneity in the final worship should be welcomed. Groups 1-3 will decide what they have to contribute in the light of their chosen activities. The fourth group could offer their Bible reading (Luke 22.39-46) with a brief comment interpreting it as a further occasion when Jesus was thrust into deep and painful thoughtfulness about his ministry. Include a period of silence for personal Lenten reflection as each person considers 'What does God want of me?'

SIGNPOSTS TO JERUSALEM

Introduction

This service can be used on any Sunday in Lent and takes its inspiration from the Catholic tradition of the 'Stations of the Cross'. Our 'stations' are called 'Signposts' and are taken from the entire ministry of Jesus. The aim is to help the congregation give thanks for Jesus Christ as healer, teacher, and friend etc. Some members of the congregation are involved in preparing the service. All but very young children can stay in church for the entire period.

Preparation

Well in advance of the service call together five groups of peoples, e.g. families, friends, etc. Give each group a task of organising a small display, and a five minute act of worship on one of the themes:

The Baptism of Jesus	Jesus the Lord
Jesus the Teacher	Jesus the Healer
	Jesus, Friend of all

In advance of the service the five groups set up the signpost-displays around the church; the themes clearly marked. Suggestions are given but they should be adapted. In the service the Leader and a further small group of mixed ages go from display to display, leading the worship planned by the groups. Decide how leadership of the worship at each signpost is to be shared.

The Festival Service

Opening sentences

As the time approached when he was to be taken up to heaven, Jesus set his face resolutely towards Jerusalem, and sent messengers ahead.

(Luke 9. 51)

Leader

'Jesus set his face resolutely towards Jerusalem'. In one sentence Luke has captured the feelings of hope, fear, promise, and inevitability as Jesus, his ministry in Galilee accomplished, turns to the capital city. If he confronts the leaders of the nation is there the hope that they may respond and re-discover the purposes of God they have set aside? Is his face resolute because already the Cross is casting its shadow over his life? In this service we trace his steps, not simply to see where he walked but to discover who he is, and the nature of his ministry both then, and now.

Several groups have prepared this service. Around us are the signposts of the journey. As some of us move from one to another we will explore the ministry of Jesus and invite you to share in the worship we offer in his name.

Prayer

Eternal God, Lord of all ages, present in all times, our faith spans the centuries to walk with Jesus in his journey of hope and fear, service and comradeship. Our steps falter as did those of his first disciples. As with them, he strides before us with a confidence and resolution we cannot share. Forgive us for our indecision and grant that as we seek to understand him better so his ministry to us may touch our hearts and minds, and bring us to deeper discipleship. Accept this our worship as a Lenten pilgrimage of faith. In Christ's Name.

Amen.

Hymn   Son of the Lord most high

During this hymn the Leader and a small group of people of mixed ages make their way to the first signpost.

Signpost One: The Baptism of Jesus

The display could include a picture of the baptism of Jesus, and of water. Include the font, baptism certificates, the Cradle Roll etc.

Leader

Our journey begins when Jerusalem seemed a long way away, and with an event which Matthew interprets as being confirmation of Jesus' calling as God's messenger.

Bible reading   Mathew 3.13-17

Reading: A Russian author once wrote:

'I asked him once, "Grandpa, what do people live for?" They live for something better to come, my friend. Let's say, there are cabinet-

11

makers. They live on, and all of them are just trash. But one day a cabinet-maker is born – such a cabinet-maker as had never been seen on this earth – there's no equal to him – he outshines everybody. The whole cabinet-making trade is changed by him – and in one jump it moves twenty years ahead. Likewise all the rest – locksmiths, say – cobblers and other working people – and peasants, too – and even the masters – they all live for something better to come.

They live a hundred – and maybe more years for a better man. Everybody, my friend, lives for something better to come.

That's why we have to be considerate of every man – Who knows what's in him, why he was born, and what he can do? Maybe he was born for our good fortune – for our greater benefit.'

(Maksim Gor'ky)

Prayer

Grant, Lord of the Church, that having been baptised in the name of Jesus we may ever be faithful to him.

Amen

The Leader and group move to the next signpost.

Signpost Two: Jesus the Lord

Display symbols or pictures of authority; e.g. crown, throne. Also symbols of Christian authority; e.g. donkey, foot-washing and pictures of the call of the disciples.

Bible reading Matthew 4.18-22

Invite someone briefly to describe how he/she became a Christian and what it means to say 'Jesus is Lord'.

Meditation

In a period of silence invite people to think about their own first steps of faith. Suggest the children think what is most important, and what they most enjoy about coming to church. Conclude the silence with the following:

Reading

He comes to us as one unknown, without a name, as of old, by the lakeside, he came to those men who knew him not. He speaks to us the same words: 'Follow thou me!' and sets us to the tasks which he has to fulfil in our time. He commands. And to those who obey him, whether they be wise or simple, he will reveal himself in the toils, the conflicts, the sufferings which they shall pass through in his fellowship, and as an ineffable mystery, they shall learn in their own experience who he is.

(Albert Schweitzer)

Hymn   Jesus calls us!

The Leader and group move to the next signpost.

Signpost Three: Jesus the Teacher

Display objects/pictures relating to school and learning. Include adult education, and ideas from the parables; e.g. a candle (light under bushel), grain (the sower).

Bible reading   Matthew 5. 21-10

Parables: *Ask previously invited members of the group to complete the sentence, 'I like the parable of Jesus about. . . best of all because it. . .' Show the objects from the parables. Invite people to identify the parables.*

Drama   *Act out one (or two) of the parables, e.g. the Sower.*

Prayer

We thank you, O God, for the teaching ministry of Jesus, for his patience with those who were slow to learn, and his simplicity which all could understand.

We need that patience, for we ourselves have been slow to learn. Give us the teachable spirit so that, as we read his words, we may understand and, having understood, may have the will to obey.

Amen

(Prayers for the Church Community)

Hymn   Tell me the stories of Jesus.   *(selected verses)*

The Leader and group move to the next signpost.

Signpost Four: Jesus the Healer

Include pictures of the healing miracles, examples of present-day healing, e.g. first aid items, pictures of hospitals, examples of medical missions.

Bible reading   Luke 5 .12-26

Prepare this as a dramatic reading. Two people read the narrative sections together, another speaks the words attributed to Jesus, and another, those of the man with leprosy, others the words of the lawyers and Pharisees.

Comment   *If available invite a doctor/nurse briefly to suggest how their work relates to their faith. Or, ask someone to say how they value the National Health Service.*

Prayer of Intercession

Lord Jesus Christ, your loving hand touched the sick and lonely to bring wholeness and calm. Present still in the skill of the surgeon, the care of the nurse, the organisation of health-care, and in simple human friendship, bring wholeness and health to all who are ill. Amen

Hymn Jesus' hands were kind hands.
During the hymn move to the next signpost.

Signpost Five: Jesus, Friend of all
Display a collage showing people of different age, colour and nationality.

Bible readings *Use different voices.*
- Luke 7. 36-38   ● Luke 9. 52-56   ● Luke 18. 15-17

Story: The Black Brotherhood
'Bang, bang! The heavy brass knocker echoed down an empty, sunny street in the city of Florence. Then there was a scamper of feet as the two young lads who had knocked, tore away as fast as they could go. Once out of sight round the next corner they doubled up with laughter. "Good for you, Giovanni!" chuckled Marc. "Shall we do it again?" But Giovanni had a better idea.

"Let's go over to the new houses they are building; the workmen will have gone home, and we can have some fun with the ladders," he suggested. So off the two boys went.

Dodging through the crowded street, the brothers came to the half-built houses. Giovanni looked cautiously about. "The foreman caught me here the other day," he said.

"Keep a look-out for me, Marco; I'm going up this ladder. I'll watch for you afterwards while you go up. Here, help me to move the plank the men have put across to stop us." Then Marco stood sentry while Giovanni began to climb. "It's a bit rickety," he called. Marco divided his attention rather anxiously between the ladder and the road down which the foreman might appear. Then somehow – he could never tell how it happened – the ladder tilted. Giovanni gave a terrified shout, clutched in vain, and fell headlong to the ground.

He did not move or cry, but lay still and white. "Giovanni! Giovanni!" Marco called, shaking him, but he could get no response. Frightened, the younger boy began to cry. One or two passers-by stopped to see what had happened; soon quite a crowd had gathered. No one seemed to know quite what to do, till someone suggested, "Run for one of the Black Brothers."

14

Off went the boy and was soon back. With him came a man strangely clothed in a long black robe and a black hood: a black mask covered his face, so that no one could recognise him. His voice was rough but not unkind.

"Now then," he said, "What's all this?" He bent over Giovanni and examined him quickly. "A broken leg, I think," he said. "Cheer up, lad" – to Marco; "We'll soon have him comfortable." Giving brief directions, he went off, but quickly returned with five other men in similar black robes, also masked. Four of the Black Brothers carried between them a kind of covered stretcher, black too. On to this they carefully lifted the injured boy. Very gently they moved off, Marco running beside them.

The Black Brothers brought their stretcher and carried Giovanni gently and easily to one small room in a back street that was his home. A Black Brother carried him up the stairs and laid him on the lumpy mattress. "There," he said, arranging the hurt leg in the most comfortable position, and bringing a drink of water. "One of us will be in to help you tomorrow about this time. Meanwhile, Marco, you must look after your brother."

Those were weary days for Giovanni. His leg was still very painful. His father was out at work all day, and Marco, though he did his best, was after all only a little boy. But every day, about six in the evening, there would be a knock at the door, and in would come one of the Black Brotherhood.

"Greetings, Giovanni!" he would say. "How's the leg today?" With strong, tender hands he would change the bandages then he would bring water, and wash Giovanni's hot face and hands. He would straighten the room, and bring food to the boy. Sometimes he would tell a story to while away the time, and always before he went he would kneel down and say a prayer. One day Giovanni caught hold of the black robe as the visitor was preparing to go. "Can't you stay a little longer today?" he said. "I do want to ask you something. Why do you wear these black masks? What is the Black Brotherhood?"

The visitor sat down on the side of the bed. "I will tell you all about it," he said. "Our real name is the Brotherhood of the Misericordia, which means the Brotherhood of the Gentle Heart. The brothers are rich men and poor men, nobles and shopkeepers, bricklayers and porters, doctors and teachers. All day long we do our own work. But at five o'clock each evening most of us meet at our church. We put on these black robes and these masks, so that no one shall know who the other is.

Then we kneel and pray for God's help. And then we go out to do God's work. We have a number of stretchers, like the one which carried you to hospital, and we go with these to people who are hurt or ill. We go, too, to the homes of sick people and look after them."

And who pays you?' asked Giovanni.

"Pay!" laughed the Brother. "Why, we take no pay. We work for love of Him who was gentle and kind. We ask no other reward."

"Who began the Black Brotherhood?" Marco asked.

"Ah, that is almost the best part of the story," said his friend. "I'll tell you. Five hundred years ago, when there were no carriages in Florence, the grand ladies were carried from place to place in these covered stretchers. The porters who carried these litters (as they were called) used to wait in the square for someone to engage them. They were rough, wild men, and they used to gamble and fight and swear.

One day a man called Pietro came as a porter. He was quite poor, but he hated the swearing and bad language; and he got some of the men to try and give up the habit."

"If we forget," he suggested, "Let us fine ourselves a farthing!" So they agreed. They did try, but in spite of trying they forgot, and presently Pietro had quite a full bag of fines. "What shall we do with the money?" the porters wondered. Pietro had a good idea.

"Let"s buy an extra litter," he suggested, "And use it to carry sick folk, or people who are hurt in street fights." Once more they all agreed; they bought the litter and took it in turns to carry it. And that is how our Brotherhood began.

But presently other people saw how splendid the work was and wanted to join. "Now we have dukes and judges and all sorts of important people as brothers, but we still have porters and poor men too. Under the black robes no one can recognise us as rich or poor."

"When I grow up I shall be a brother," Giovanni decided.

"Perhaps so," his friend agreed. "But remember, to be a brother, you must always be ready, not only at five o'clock but always. For if there is a special need, we sound the great bell, and when it rings, all the brothers, whatever they are doing, leave their work or their homes and come at once to help."

"My leg is almost well," Giovanni said. "When I can walk could I join the Brotherhood at once?"

"Not quite at once," said his friend. "You must wait till you are older. But I think you could begin to practise for it at once. Do you know what I mean?"

Giovanni was quiet for a minute. "I think so," he said. "Is it easy?"

"Not always," said the Brother. "I'll tell you one more story, and then I must go. Once there was a man who was a builder's foreman. He had a lot of trouble with boys who would come to his building in the evening and steal his sand and climb his ladders and spoil his work. He warned them often, and they took no notice. One day he caught a boy trespassing, and gave him a good beating. The man was angry – perhaps too angry; but the boy deserved it. Well, this man was a member of the Brotherhood; and several evenings later he was called to an accident, and found. . ."

Giovanni was listening open-mouthed. He ended the sentence as the Brother paused. "Found it was the same boy! And you never said anything about it being my own fault. It was you, wasn't it?"

The Brother was at the door. "Yes," he said. "Don't tell anyone, lad. And yet it was not I, but the Black Brotherhood that came to your aid." He corrected himself again. "No, not even the Brotherhood, but the Lord of the Brotherhood".'

from 'Stories for the 8-13's' (NCEC)

Hymn   One there is above all others   or
What a friend we have in Jesus

Prayer

No shadow darkens the friendship you offer to us, Lord Jesus Christ. No trivial mood or passing fancy alters the constancy of your compassion. No wind of change blows, first hot then cold, to blight the love you offer. You call us your friends and your deed is as good as your word.

Thanksgiving, praise and adoration is our glad response to you, our friend and Lord.   Amen

(Prayers for the Church Community)

In silence following the prayer, arrange for a man in first century dress, and carrying two pieces of 'timber', to walk slowly down the aisle and place them at the front in a manner suggesting a cross. The 'timber' may be polystyrene or thin lathes, covered with painted paper. Ideally find someone the members do not know or provide headgear that obscures his face. No comment should be made and when he has gone, maintain the silence as long as is reasonable.

Hymn   Praise to the Holiest in the height.

Benediction

GOD'S MOMENT

Introduction

The Palm Sunday story portrays symbolic events on one day in Jesus' life. Luke gives more details than the other gospel writers and includes Jesus' reaction on seeing Jerusalem from the heights above the city. Jesus attributes its eventual destruction to an inability to 'recognise God's moment'. If they had responded to the insights of the prophets, or fully shared the praise of the Psalmists, the history of Israel could have been very different. Even on Palm Sunday how few recognised the significance of a Messiah on a donkey, and how many missed God's moment as they turned their songs of praise into cries for Jesus' death. This service looks at some of these missed opportunities leading us to ask if we are any more attentive in our time.

Preparation

The young children come into church with palms or branches (prepared in advance) during the first hymn. They leave later and return towards the end to distribute palm crosses to the congregation. *(Palm crosses can be obtained at a relatively small cost from Charles Ferris, Bishopgate Works, Staines Road, Hounslow, Middlesex, TW4 5DN).*

A choral reading of the Palm Sunday story is a major feature of the service. Using a number of voices it is read in full, early in the service, and then various sections are repeated as the service continues. The choral reading group and other readers should be in their place before the service begins and remain for the whole service, standing to read at a silent signal from the Leader.

The Festival Service

Call to worship

Rejoice, rejoice, daughter of Zion,
shout aloud, daughter of Jerusalem;
for see, your king is coming to you,
his cause won, his victory gained,
humble and mounted on an ass,
on a foal, the young of a she-ass.
He shall speak peaceably to every nation,
and his rule shall extend from sea to sea,
from the River to the ends of the earth.

(from Zechariah 9. 9-10)

Hymn   All glory, laud and honour

During this hymn the younger children process into church with 'palm-leaves'. These can be made of rolls of paper split at the top, or be small branches from natural trees.

Leader   Pictures and symbols crowd into our minds on Palm Sunday. The people wave palm branches as they see their king enter Jerusalem. But what a strange king he is! When most kings choose powerful horses for victory rides, this king rides a donkey, a colt. It was a deliberate choice. What message lies behind that choice? Let's hear the story as Luke tells it.

Choral reading

Five voices are needed for this reading. Apart from VOICE 2 (an individual male) they could be individual voices or groups. Include younger and older people.

VOICE 1	With that Jesus went forward and began the ascent to Jerusalem. As he approached Bethphage and Bethany at the hill called Olivet, he sent two of the disciples with these instructions:
VOICE 2	'Go to the village opposite; as you enter it you will find tethered there a colt which no one has yet ridden. Untie it and bring it here. If anyone asks you why you are untying it, say, Our Master needs it.'
VOICE 1	The two went on their errand and found it as he had told them: and while they were untying the colt, its owners asked,
VOICE 3	'Why are you untying that colt.'

19

VOICE 1	They answered,
VOICE 4	'Our Master needs it.'
VOICE 1	So they brought the colt to Jesus. Then they threw their cloaks on the colt, for Jesus to mount, and they carpeted the road with them as he went on his way. And now, as he approached the descent from the Mount of Olives, the whole company began to sing aloud the praises of God for all the great things they had seen:
ALL	'Blessings on him who comes as king in the name of the Lord! Peace in heaven, glory in highest heaven!'
VOICE 1	Some Pharisees who were in the crowd said to him,
VOICE 5	'Master, reprimand your disciples.'
VOICE 1	He answered,
VOICE 2	'I tell you, if my disciples keep silence the stones will shout aloud.'
VOICE 1	When he came in sight of the city, he wept over it and said,
VOICE 2	'If only you had known, on this great day, the way that leads to peace! But no; it is hidden from your sight. For a time will come upon you, when your enemies will set up siege-works against you; they will encircle you and hem you in at every point; they will bring you to the ground, you and your children within your walls, and will not leave you one stone standing on another, because you did not recognise God's moment when it came.
VOICE 1	Then he went into the temple and began driving out the traders, with these words:
VOICE 2	'Scripture says, "My house shall be a house of prayer"; but you have made it a robbers' cave.'

Leader Jesus rebuked the people: 'You did not recognise God's moment when it came.' But *what* is God's moment? *When* is God's moment? How do we recognise it so as to find peace rather than war? Within our praise and worship today that is the question we are asking.

Prayer

A donkey king! Were there those who laughed?

20

Did some scorn?
How many turned their heads, embarrassed?
What of the anger of those who saw a sacred prophecy abused?

But now, O Lord, with the hindsight of the cross, it makes sense to us,
so we are glad:

    glad of the applause of the crowd who trusted their first reactions
    and welcomed their donkey king,
    glad of the shouts of little children caught up in a sense of
    celebration,
    glad that there were those who glimpsed, fleetingly, the nature of a
    king who straddled a donkey.

Donkey King, we join the throng, we raise a voice of childlike praise,
we glimpse the secret of your reign. Welcome to our Jerusalem!

                                      Amen

Leader   If we are looking for God's moment in our own lives we can
find clues in the Palm Sunday story. Whatever else it was, it was a
moment of praise. Does God's moment occur in our joyous worship?

Choral reading

VOICE 1   And now, as he approached the descent from the
                Mount of Olives, the whole company began to sing
                aloud the praises of God for all the great things they
                had seen:

ALL   'Blessings on him who comes as king in the name of
                the Lord! Peace in heaven, glory in highest heaven!'

Praises *Sing joyful songs or hymns preferably led by a lively group. Choose
choruses or short songs of praise. If drums, tambourines, etc. are available make
sure these are distributed to the children and others before the service, so they
can join in immediately.*

Reading or **Solo** *(the words and tune are in several hymn books)*

    When, in our music, God is glorified,
    and adoration leaves no room for pride,
    it is as though the whole creation cried:
      Alleluia!

    And did not Jesus sing a psalm that night
    when utmost evil strove against the Light?
    then let us sing, for whom he won the fight:
      Alleluia!

Let every instrument be tuned for praise!
Let all rejoice who have a voice to raise!
And may God give us faith to sing always:
Alleluia!   (F. Pratt Green)

Hymn   Give me joy in my heart

Leader
Praise the Lord, all his people!
The gentle king is coming to rule!
The Lord of love is visiting his people!
Kindness is enthroned, and humility wears a crown!
The face of God is wreathed in smiles,
    and we are his people!
Praise the Lord, all his people!

Leader   Moments of praise can become moments of God, and so can quieter moments of reflection and thought. *Monica Furlong* remembers just such moments.

Reader   During the two years just before and after I was twenty I had two experieces which led to religious conversion. The first occurred when I was waiting at a bus stop on a wet afternoon. It was opposite the Odeon cinema, outside the station, and I was surrounded by people, shops, cars. A friend was with me. All of a sudden, for no apparent reason, everything looked different. Everything I could see shone, vibrated, throbbed with joy and with meaning. I knew that it had done this all along, and would go on doing it, but that usually I couldn't see it. It was all over in a minute or two. I climbed on the bus, saying nothing to my friend – it seemed impossible to explain – and sat stunned with astonishment and happiness.
    The second experience occurred some months later. I left my office at lunch-time, stopped at a small Greek cafe in Fleet Street to buy some rolls and fruit, and walked up Chancery Lane. It was an August day, quite warm but cloudy, with the sun glaringly, painfully bright behind the clouds. I had a strong sense that something was about to happen. I sat on a seat in the garden of Lincoln's Inn waiting for whatever it was to occur. The sun behind the clouds grew brighter and brighter, the clouds assumed a shape which fascinated me, and between one moment and the next, although no word had been uttered, I felt myself spoken to. I was aware of being regarded in love, of being wholly accepted, accused,

forgiven, all at once. The joy of it was the greatest I had ever known in my life. I felt I had been born for this moment and had marked time till it occurred.

Leader   Was there such a moment for a small group of people on the first day of a certain week, in the city of Jerusalem long ago when they glimpsed the real meaning of kingship, and God's nature as better understood?

Choral reading

VOICE 1	'Why are you untying that colt.'
VOICE 2	They answered,
VOICE 4	'Our Master needs it.'
VOICE 1	So they brought the colt to Jesus. Then they threw their cloaks on the colt, for Jesus to mount, and they carpeted the road with them as he went on his way.

Leader   A young child – about 6 years old – wrote a prayer. She knew God's moment.

Reading   *(a young child)*

Dear God. I just feel good knowing that you are everywhere. That's all.

Hymn   What means this eager, anxious throng
or, Wise men seeking Jesus.

A modern parable   *This could be read by one person but would be more effective read by two, though still using reported speech. The first few lines are set out for two people, the rest of the parable can readily be used in the same way.*

VOICE 1	I saw God the other day. I did really. I just looked up and there he was, sitting on the edge of a cloud, dangling his legs. I said, 'Hello, God, how are you?'
VOICE 2	'Not so bad,' he said. 'How'd you know it was me?'
VOICE 1	I said, 'Well, I just guessed, really. Seeing you sitting up there on a cloud – wasn't anyone else it could be.'
VOICE 2	'Rubbish,' said God. 'Could've been anybody – spaceman, steeplejack, window-cleaner, lift-attendant – anybody with a head for heights'.
VOICE 1	'Yes, but not just sitting up there on a cloud,' I

said.

He was quiet for a minute – thinking. Then he moved round and propped himself up on his elbows and peered at me over the edge of the cloud.

VOICE 2   'What else?' he said.

VOICE 1   'Well, you look like God,' I said, 'With that old wrinkled face and long white beard. You're what I've always imagined you to be. Who else could you be?'

VOICE 2   'Father Christmas,' he suggested.

VOICE 1   'Don't be daft,' I said. 'Nobody believes in Father Christmas.'

VOICE 2   'Does anyone believe in me?' he asked.

VOICE 1   'Well,' I said, 'some do, some don't.'

VOICE 2   So he asked, 'Those who do – what do they say?'

VOICE 1   'They look at the world,' I said. 'And they see the beauty and order of nature, and they reckon it couldn't have happened by accident. Must be God.'

VOICE 2   'I see,' said God. 'And those who don't?'

VOICE 1   'They look at the world as well,' I told him. 'They look at war and human misery, homelessness, pollution. They reckon if God existed, it wouldn't happen.'

VOICE 2   'I see,' said God. 'You know their trouble, don't you? It's not me they don't believe in, it's themselves. I mean to say – I've given them the power to put it right. They just won't use it.'

VOICE 1   'What power's that?' I asked.

VOICE 2   'They know right from wrong,' he said. 'That's all they need.'

VOICE 1   'Not willpower?' I asked.

VOICE 2   'Ah,' he said, and I'm certain he winked at me. 'They have to ask for that.'

VOICE 1   'Ask for it?'

VOICE 2   'Well, I can't give it to them if they don't want it,' he said. 'It'd be like stepping in and clearing up the mess myself. I couldn't do that now, could I?'

VOICE 1   'Why not?' I asked him.

VOICE 2   'Well. . .' he said, and he winked again, and smiled. 'It'd leave 'em with nothing to do, wouldn't it. They'd have such an easy time of it, they *still* wouldn't believe

	in me.'
VOICE 1	Then he disappeared, and I thought about what he had said, and I remembered the smile and the wink, and wondered if he was joking. Suddenly, he came back. He stood on the cloud, his face like thunder. He cupped his hands, and he called out to the world below. . .
VOICE 2	'BESIDES – IT'S YOUR MESS!'

Hymn Trotting, trotting through Jerusalem
or other modern children's hymn for Palm Sunday.

During this hymn any children for whom a full service is too long should process out, still with their palms.

Amongst any activities prepared for them during the rest of the service they should be made ready to distribute the palm crosses to the congregation on their return.

Choral reading

VOICE 2	'If only you had known, on this great day, the way that leads to peace! But no; it is hidden from your sight. For a time will come upon you, when your enemies will set up siege-works against you, they will encircle you and hem you in at every point; they will bring you to the ground, you and your children within your walls, and will not leave you one stone standing on another, because you did not recognise God's moment when it came.'
VOICE 1	Then he went into the temple and began driving out the traders, with these words:
VOICE 2	'Scripture says: "My house shall be a house of prayer;" but you have made it a robbers' cave.'

Address

Introduction: Both the modern parable and the Palm Sunday story bring together the humility and the judgment of God. The gentle king who refuses the military trapping of a triumphal entry and chooses a donkey-entry instead nonetheless goes straight to the temple with righteous indignation.

The following points can be made:
In John's gospel the cleansing of the temple is put at the very beginning of Jesus' ministry. The Synoptics put it on Palm Sunday. In both cases the message is

clear: the first arena for the declaration of the rule of God is the temple. The church is cleansed before the nation can hear the truth. What does that say to our contemporary church and nation?

Jesus' message is more than that worship must have priority over commerce. The traders were operating in the only court of the temple where Gentiles could worship.

Their presence was a denial of the universality of faith, and the love of God for all peoples.

Hymn Almighty Father, who for us Thy Son didst give
or other hymn on social justice and true worship.

Reading *(or use part as an illustration in the address).*
This is the Church of my dreams —
The Church of the warm heart,
Of the open mind,
Of the adventurous spirit;
The Church that cares,
That heals hurt lives.
That comforts old people,
That challenges youth;
That knows no divisions of culture or class;
No frontiers, geographical or social,
The Church that enquires as well as avers,
That looks forward as well as backward;
The Church of the Master,
The Church of the people;
High as the ideals of Jesus,
Low as the humblest human;
A working Church,
A worshipping Church,
A winsome Church;
A Church that interprets truth in terms of truth;
That inspires courage for this life and hope for the life to come:
A Church of courage;
A Church of all good men —
A Church of the living God

Anon

Hymn Ride on! Ride on!
During this hymn the younger children return and distribute palm crosses to the congregation. The music should continue until the task is complete.

26

Prayer

Lord Jesus Christ, time and again you take us by surprise.
Kings are born in palaces,
> but you make your first appearance in a stable bed.

Important people stand on their dignity and expect others to give them pride of place,
> but you slip into life to become one of the people, and even wash your disciple's feet.

Martial bands and mighty processions are the way others plan victory parades,
> but you come quietly riding the gentlest beast of all.

Where will you go now, Lord Jesus Christ?
> Will you let them push you around instead of fighting back?
> Will you watch friends betray you without pointing an accusing finger at them?
> Will you let them take you without a struggle?
> Will you even let them put you on a cross, Lord, with pain and hurt?

Lord Jesus, fill our moments with your eternal moment.
Lead us to the peace which no one else can offer.   Amen

Benediction

LET LOOSE IN THE WORLD

Introduction

Jesus Christ was born into one nation and at a specific period of time. Therefore, he was restricted in movement and contact. The resurrection released him from these restrictions of time and place. He is now the universal Lord who speaks to all times and is present in every place.

This Easter service takes its theme from an imaginary conversation between a disciple of Jesus and a Roman centurion immediately after the crucifixion. The centurion suggests that Jesus is 'let loose in the world' and thus anticipates the resurrection. The service celebrates the way in which the risen Lord has been released to be present not only for each individual and the church, but for the whole world, and for all time. The service thus has three parts. Resurrection sets Jesus free:

- to meet each individual
- to be with his Church in every place
- to be the Saviour of the world

Preparation

Two people are needed for the opening item and arrangements made for them to be heard even if not seen. Various readers are required including three for the testimonies, and three to describe missionary conviction. One member of the church is invited to give a personal testimony to Christ's presence in his/her life.

A large map of Great Britain is needed and coloured stickers. Some members should be alerted to respond quickly to the request for names of Christian worshippers in other churches. The children's leaders should plan the Easter cards, suitable envelopes, and stamps.

The Festival Service

As the musical voluntary dies away allow a short silence. The first two speakers should preferably be unseen or be in a dark corner of the church. But they must be heard.

PROCULA   Centurion, were you at the killing of that teacher, today?

LONGINUS   Yes, my lady.

PROCULA   Tell me about his death.

LONGINUS   It is hardly fit hearing for you, my lady. . .

PROCULA   Do not tell it all, then, but tell me what he said.

LONGINUS   The people were mocking him at first, and he prayed to God to forgive them. He said: 'Father, forgive them, for they know not what they do. . .'

PROCULA   Was he suffering much?

LONGINUS   No, lady. He wasn't a strong man. The scourging must have nearly killed him. I thought he was dead by noon, and then suddenly he began to sing in a loud voice that he was giving back his spirit to God. I looked to see God come to take him. He died singing. Truly, lady, that man was the Son of God, if one may say that. . .

PROCULA   What do you think the man believed, centurion?

LONGINUS   He believed he was God, they say.

PROCULA   What do you think of that claim?

LONGINUS   If a man believes anything up to the point of dying on the cross for it, he will find others to believe it.

PROCULA   Do you believe it?

LONGINUS   He was a fine young fellow, my lady; not past middle age. And he was all alone and defied all the Jews and all the Romans, and, when we had done with him, he was a poor broken-down thing, dead on the cross.

PROCULA   Do you think he is dead?

LONGINUS   No lady I don't.

PROCULA   Then where is he?

LONGINUS   Let loose in the world, lady, where neither Roman nor Jew can stop his truth.

(John Masefield)

Leader   You have nothing to fear. I know you are looking for Jesus who was crucified. He is not here; he has been raised again as he said he would be. Go quickly and tell his disciples: 'He has been raised from the dead and is going on before you. . .' That is what I have to tell you.

(adapted from Matthew 28. 5-7)

Hymn   Christ the Lord is risen today.

Prayer

> Welcome, Lord Jesus Christ,
>   no borders contain you,
>   nothing can fence you in,
>   you leap the boundaries that try to restrict.
> You are the Lord of space and distance.
>
> Welcome, Lord Jesus Christ,
>   no changing season robs you of your power,
>   nothing in day or night can hold you down,
>   you take the passing years in your stride.
> You are the Lord of time.
>
> Welcome, Lord Jesus Christ,
>   no flags of nations curb your style,
>   nothing of race or culture keeps you back,
>   you speak to every needful human heart.
> You are the Lord of humankind
>
> Welcome, ever-welcome Lord.   Amen

Leader   For three years Jesus lived and worked in one country, meeting only a limited number of people. With only a few exceptions, he met only Jewish people. That was the price of incarnation. The resurrection released him. He was let loose in the world. Now, the risen Lord spans the earth and leaps across the centuries. That is the truth we celebrate this Easter Day. We give thanks to God for the Lord who is always going on before us. That is true for each individual, for the Christian community, for the whole world, and to the end of time.

Arrange for different people to read the following items as the leader introduces them.

JESUS IS SET FREE TO MEET EACH INDIVIDUAL. Listen to the testimony of those who have met him. Paul never saw Jesus in the flesh but he makes his own testimony.

Testimony 1 (Paul)   1 Corinthians 15. 3-8

Leader Hsu T'ien Hsien was a minister of a small rural Presbyterian church in South Taiwan when he was arrested for alleged involvement in a human rights rally. From his prison cell on September 6th 1981, he testified to the risen Christ.

Testimony 2 (Hsu T'ien Hsien)

If the Lord is in prison with me,
  what do I fear?
Lonely and solitary though I am,
  I believe,
  I praise,
  I give thanks.
If the Lord is in prison with me,
  who do I grieve?
The Lord knows my trouble and pain,
  with him I entrust my heart and my all.
  I believe,
  I rejoice,
  I sing.

Leader Martin Luther King affirmed the faith that we rise with Christ.

Testimony 3 (Martin Luther King)

So I say to you, seek God and discover him and make him a power in your life. Without him all of our efforts turn to ashes and our sunrise into darkest nights. Without him life is a meaningless drama with the decisive scenes missing. But with him we are able to rise from the fatigue of despair to the buoyancy of hope. With him we are able to rise from the midnight of desperation to the daybreak of joy.

Leader A young Dutch child grasped the truth and wrote a prayer. We share it now. *A seven/eight year old reads.*

Jesus, you're alive!
Not as you were alive in Galilee with your friends.
Then only the people who met you could talk to you –
but now everybody can.
I'm talking to you and you're with me;
friends of yours all over the world
are talking to you now, this very minute,
and you're with them.

That's what I like about you
– Alive for everyone.

Testimony 4 *Invite a member of the congregation to give a brief personal testimony of Christ's presence.*

Leader An ancient hymn writer – *the Venerable Bede* – invites us to share his testimony as we sing.

Hymn Sing we triumphant hymns of praise *(or another hymn stressing personal conviction about the risen Lord).*

Leader JESUS IS SET FREE TO BE WITH HIS CHURCH IN EVERY PLACE.
At this very moment and all over the country women and men, girls and boys are meeting, like us, to greet the Lord who rose from the tomb.

Turn to the large map of Great Britain. Invited people stand and tell of friends who will be celebrating Easter in church; e.g. 'I know James and Sarah Smith and their children, William and Tracey. They will be in church in Manchester'. For each name stick previously prepared labels, marked with the name on the map on the mentioned town. Invite others in the congregation to tell of people they know will be in church e.g. 'Philip in Nottingham', 'Jack and Sandra in Bournemouth'. Mark the towns. Speed is important, geographical accuracy is not. Aim to show the church of Christ at worship across the nation. Give envelopes of a size appropriate to receive the Easter cards the children will make, to some of the members. Invite them to write the address of their friends.

Leader Our map shows us the Church we know. It meets in many places we do not know. Together the unknown and the known make up the Community of the Resurrection. We cannot greet all our Christian friends this morning but we can greet some. The children in the church will help us.

Invite the children (say, up to 10 years) to move to another room and make Easter cards bearing a greeting from your church. Shortage of time means that either the children will need to have begun the task the previous week, or the leaders will have to bring part-completed cards. The children will return later with the cards.

Leader JESUS IS SET FREE TO BE THE SAVIOUR OF THE WORLD.

Hymn Christ is the world's Light. He and none other.

Leader The pattern of world mission changes; the motive remains the same. The early church expressed it thus:

Reader 1   Matthew 28.16-20

Leader   On August 10th 1796 it was expressed like this:

Reader 2   'August the 10th 1796, at six in the morning, we weighed anchor and hoisted our missionary flag. . . three doves argent on a purple field bearing olive branches in their bills. The morning was serene, and a gentle breeze blew from the W.N.W; few vessels were stirring on the river; all was still and quiet. The hymn, "Jesus, at Thy command we launch into the deep" was sung by upwards of a hundred voices. . . the sailors in the ships we passed heard with silent astonishment, and our friends who lined the banks of the river waved their hands and bade us a last adieu. . .'

That is an extract from the journal of *The Duff* which carried thirty missionaries from London. After an arduous journey 18 missionaries landed at Tahiti, nine at Tonga and a solitary brave man on the Marquesas. Their united purpose was to preach the glorious gospel of the blessed God. They knew that the risen Christ was with them.

Leader   In our own time we express it in different words. The world church as one inter-dependent family. No longer are there 'senders' and 'receivers'. All send and all receive. Mission agencies encourage churches across the world to share insights, and co-operate in demonstrating God's love for all, and particularly for the poor and disadvantaged. The same risen Lord goes before us in service and love. A hymn-writer has expressed it thus:

1   Once from a European shore
    men sailed to find and rule the earth,
    to purchase slaves with bales of cloth
or take a civilising law.
Give thanks that some upon that tide,
    with faith and failings like our own,
    went out to preach in lands unknown
that Christ for every man had died.

2   Give thanks that with the tangled strands,
    of empire, honour, greed and love,
    a single world God's Spirit wove
from earth's long separated lands.

And now that all mankind must face,
the dread and hope of being one,
give thanks again that Christ is known
in every continent and race.

3 A great community of hope,
by reconciling love reborn,
today from all the earth is drawn –
God's pageant and kaleidoscope.
Give thanks that treasures long prepared,
– the wisdom, insight, gifts and grace
of every culture, age and place –
in Christ can now be seen and shared.

Brian Wren

Prayer

Risen Lord, yours is the power that reaches every human heart. You
understand our lives and speak to us in both our joy and our distress.
You match your step to ours so that you become companion and
friend.

Risen Lord, yours is the power that sweeps through the Church. You
come to bless and judge. You come in compassion and leadership.
You come to change us so that we are better instruments to fulfil your
good purpose.

Risen Lord, yours is the power that stretches to the ends of the earth.
You span the nations and go before us in our mission and service.
Yours is the truth we share.

Risen Lord, come with power this Easter Day. Touch our hearts.
Enliven your Church. Make the kingdoms of the world the Kingdom
of our God.   Amen

Hymn   Come, let us join our cheerful songs.

Sermon

*Briefly suggest that all that Jesus did within the restrictions of his earthly
ministry has been released into all the world and across the generations by his
resurrection. Draw on local experience of the work of Christ in the Church and
also on wider international work (missionary agencies, International Bible
Reading Associaton, Christian Aid etc).*

34

Hymn Come, Thou long-expected Jesus

The children rejoin the adults. After the hymn show the cards they have made, put them into envelopes, stamped ready for posting, and commission people to post them.

Leader The Church celebrates Easter Day – the gift of God to us in Christ. The Lord who died has broken free to fill all things. He came to us in our need and now we see him in his glory. Thanks be to God!

Bible reading 1 Corinthians 15. 20-28

Hymn Christ is alive! Let Christians sing.

Benediction

Acknowledgements

The editor and publishers gratefully acknowledge permission to reproduce the following copyright material:

Paul Carrigan:
Extract from *Something to Say* used by permission of Sheffield Diocesan Education Committee.

Albert Schweitzer:
From *Quest for the Historical Jesus* used by permission of A & C Black (Publishers) Ltd.

Fred Pratt Green:
From *When in Man's Music God is Glorified* reproduced by permission of Stainer & Bell Ltd.

Richard Adams:
From *So God Said To Me* reproduced by permission of author.

John Masefield:
From *The Trial of Jesus* used by permission of Society of Authors as literary representatives of estate of John Masefield.

Hsu T'ien Hsien:
From *Testimonies of Faith* used by permission of World Alliance of Reformed Churches.

Anon:
From *Children's Prayers* ©re02 1981 used by permission of Lion Publishing.

Martin Luther King Jr:
From *The Words of Martin Luther King Jr* selected by Coretta Scott King. © 1958, 1963, 1964, 1967 by Martin Luther King Jr used by permission of Joan Doves.

Brian Wren:
From *Once from a European Shore* reprinted by permission of Oxford University Press.

We are grateful for permission to quote from the *New English Bible* (Oxford and Cambridge University Presses) © 1970.

While every effort has been made to secure permission, we may have failed in a few cases to trace or contact the copyright holder. We apologise for any apparent negligence.